To: Liz Homola

From:

Liz Fenwick

ISBN: 978-1-970146-09-7

Manufactured in the United States of America.

Published by
McCoral Publishing
Audubon, PA, United States

Positive Mindset, Self-Awareness, Perseverance

A Guide to Thrive with Learning Differences / ADHD

Book #1

by Marc Hoffman

Download FREE WORKBOOK
with printable activities:

marchoffman.net

TABLE OF CONTENTS

INTRODUCTION

You can do anything!

Having a learning difference (LD) does not change that. Your diagnosis may feel scary, but it does not change a single thing about who you are. Your diagnosis is a good thing! It is the on-ramp for your road to success. It can point you toward the strategies and tools that will work for you.

I have years of experience helping kids with LD/ADHD succeed. Before that, I spent years struggling, and eventually succeeding, as a student myself.

These experiences have taught me a lot. I wrote this book to support kids with LD navigate their own experiences, and to help parents and educators establish a common language between generations.

My hope is that after reading this book, you will have a different perspective on the LD experience: one of empowerment and opportunity. Whether I get to work with you personally, or connect with you through a speaking engagement, Eye to Eye, or the pages of this book, my goal is the same – I want to help.

I am excited and humbled by the thought that this book will help others who are where I have been, and can reassure you on your journey to a rich and fulfilling life.

Marc Hoffman

I dedicate this book to all the parents
providing unwavering support to their child
who thinks differently,
especially my Mom,
who always praised the effort and not the
outcome.

WELCOME

The Basics

- Meet Marc -

Hi!

I am Marc Hoffman.

I have a Learning Difference (LD) and Attention Deficit and Hyperactivity Disorder (ADHD).

Some call it a learning disability, but I call it a learning difference.

I am...

- ✓ creative
- ✓ adaptive
- ✓ empathetic
- ✓ determined
- ✓ resourceful.

I also...

✓ am not a great reader

✓ have trouble spelling

✓ cannot memorize rote information such as the times table

✓ struggle to follow directions

✓ have a limited attention span.

Does any of this sound familiar? Think about what you are good at and what you struggle with. We will come back to this in a bit.

Name: _____

I AM GOOD AT...

Being a kid with a learning difference was difficult for me, so I have dedicated my life to empowering kids who learn differently.

I travel all over the country and speak about my experiences.

When I thought about writing this book, I felt excited because I knew that sharing my experiences growing up with a learning difference could really help others.

But I also felt scared about writing a whole book. I told you I do not spell well.

But you know what?

I did it!

One sentence at a time.

As a kid, school was always hard for me. It was a place where I failed, never succeeded.

Back in second grade, our class play was about the Pilgrims coming to America.

All the kids in the class had a part:

Pilgrims, Native Americans, the Captain of the Mayflower... and me.

I was... Plymouth Rock.

I was not able to memorize the lines.

So, I had the only non-speaking role.

SEE... TRUE STORY!

Most kids with a learning difference have a Plymouth Rock story.

Do you have a story just like mine?

Do you want to tell me about it?

_____

_____

_____

_____

_____

_____

_____

_____

_____

Life with a learning difference is hard work, but I can tell you the work is worth it.

In the end, my struggles made me stronger and led to my success!

And I promise, the pride and esteem you earn from overcoming obstacles lasts a lifetime.

MY

SUCCESS

IS A

RESULT

OF

MY LD,

NOT *IN SPITE* OF MY LD.

I spend my days helping kids who learn differently.

I love my job! I get to work with amazing kids like Josh, Jill and Tim.

I have a plan to help each of them.

I will share with them (and you) the things I learned as a kid that helped me survive and start feeling like a success!

Why not join us and find out if you have things in common with them.

I developed three **Success Elements**, which helped me on my journey.

These elements help the kids I support become the best they can be, not only in class but in life in general.

Before we talk more about the success elements, here are a few key takeaways:

✓ When I say LD, it includes ADHD as well. In other words, this book is for kids with LD and/or ADHD.

✓ My LD helped me find my passion to inspire and empower kids who learn differently.

✓ Life with LD can be difficult. But I have a plan for you to learn to succeed and do well.

THREE SUCCESS ELEMENTS

- ✓ **POSITIVE MINDSET**
- ✓ **SELF-AWARENESS**
- ✓ **PERSEVERANCE**

POSITIVE MINDSET:

Think The Best

- Meet Josh -

Let's meet Josh.

Josh is 14 years old and in 8th grade. He is a great athlete! Josh also enjoys video games and hanging out with his friends.

School is hard for Josh. He is a smart and kind kid, but he struggles in class.

Josh often gets stuck, confused, and upset. Believe me, I understand. I have been there. That is how I felt much of the time back when I was in class.

Josh and his parents just learned that he has a learning difference.

Just as I did, Josh is questioning his ability to be successful. He is worried that he may not get into a college or even finish high school.

When I was Josh's age, I had the same worries.

"Glad to see you, Josh.
Tell me, how is school
going?"

"Not well. I really do not
like it. I get bad grades in
a lot of subjects."

"So, school is not much
fun for you these days?"

"Not at all. It seems a lot of kids in my class do not struggle like I do.

Their grades are better than mine. But even when I try my best, getting good grades is still so hard for me. Most of the time, I don't feel smart."

"I get it, Josh. A lot of kids with a learning difference feel that way in class."

"But should you decide how 'smart' a person is based only on grades?

Think about everything you know, and all the things you can do. Do you really think that you're not smart?"

"Well..."

"O.K. Let me ask you in
a different way.

What is it that makes you
think you are not as smart
as the others in your class?"

"I can't learn like they do."

23

"You mean you learn differently. Feeling that way sounds like a tough spot to be in day after day."

"I do not think I have it in me to do this a day more!"

"There are lots of kids who feel just as you do."

"You keep saying 'learning difference.' I always hear it called a disability."

"I hear a lot of that as well. But I do not see learning differences as a disability. Let me tell you what I think a learning difference does and does not mean."

LEARNING DIFFERENCE

~~LEARNING DISABILITY~~

"Learning difference, to me, means I am...

- ✓ creative
- ✓ an "out-of-the-box" thinker
- ✓ able to size up a situation quickly.

- ✗ It **DOES NOT** mean I am not smart.

- ✗ It **DOES NOT** mean that I am lazy.

- ✗ It **DOES NOT** mean I cannot learn. I can learn in a different way, it just might take me longer in some areas.

- ✗ It **DOES NOT** mean I cannot do what I want with my life.

"The father of theoretical physics had a learning difference."

"Albert Einstein? No way!"

"Yes. So did Thomas Edison."

"Wow! I had no idea! They were really smart guys!"

"Everybody is a genius. But If you judge a fish by its ability to climb a tree, it will live its whole life believing that it is stupid."

"In fact, I bet you already work much harder than the rest of your class."

"Yes, I do. But it still does not show in my grades."

"You do not have to measure your success with only your grades. Your ability to work hard will help you throughout your whole life."

"That's easy for you
to say. You're already
successful."

"Yes, I am successful. But I did
not always feel like that when
I was your age. I did not have
good grades. In fact, I almost
failed 8th grade."

"You did? Really?"

"Yes, I almost did. My modest 8th grade goal was to make it to 9th grade."

Dear Burt and Judy Hoffman,

We are not sending you a 1991-1992 contract for Marc at this time because the faculty has grave doubts about his ability to perform satisfactorily in our 9th grade program. He failed three semester exams and two courses in January.

Should Marc fail three courses in June, he will, by school policy, not be able to return.

Sincerely,

Mr. L,
Head of Middle School

"Wow, that is rough! What happened? Did you make it to 9th grade?"

"Well, I was really scared. My mind was filled with self-doubt.

I felt like a failure. I failed almost every class that year, but I did make it to 9th grade.

Then, I finished high school, graduated from college, and even earned a Master's degree. Do you want to know what changed everything for me?"

"I met a new friend, Rick. He was in a wheelchair because of a car accident. But he always had a positive outlook on life.

When Rick asked me how things were going, I complained to him about my classes.

I told him I was thinking about giving up on school."

"Not being able to walk
must be hard."

"It must be, Josh. Rick told me
that right after his accident,
life was not easy.

But he realized that he had
a choice: Feel sorry for himself
because he could not walk
or be grateful that he was
alive. He planned to become
a doctor."

"Every day when Rick faced a difficulty, he reminded himself of this choice. He tried not to dwell on the things he could not change and worked hard to keep focused on the things he wanted to achieve.

Rick told me he was the captain of the paralympic basketball team."

"He was on a basketball team!"

"Yes, he just learned to play in a different way. Just like how I learned to study in a different way. I had to find out what worked for me.

Rick was a great basketball player. He had a lot going for him, and I realized, so did I."

"So what did you do?"

"It was as if a switch had
turned on in my head.

I realized if I could control
how I perceived my abilities,
I could influence my destiny."

"In the past, I saw my LD as a bad thing that made me less than others. I was ready to give up on school because I allowed my failures in class to determine my self-image. And I spent more time feeling sorry for myself than pushing through the tasks in front of me.

When I focused on having a **positive mindset**, I took **positive actions**, and slowly, things started to improve!"

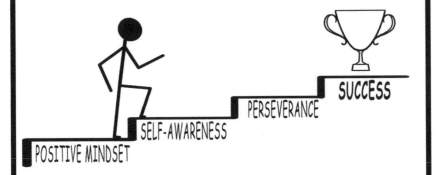

POSITIVE MINDSET

SELF-AWARENESS

PERSEVERANCE

SUCCESS

"But it can be so hard."

"Definitely. I am not saying it is easy to stay **positive**, but even when I have a bad day, I work hard to come back to a positive mindset.

Do not forget: progress is not a straight line. Setbacks don't mean we are not moving towards our goals! Just try your hardest and never give up, no matter how tough things get."

"Can you tell me a bit more about yourself, Josh? What are some skills that you can share with me?"

"Well, I am bad at school. We know that."

"How about we focus on your **strengths**, which are the things you are good at, not **weaknesses**, which are the things you do not feel like you do well."

"I just realized that my answer sounded really negative. I need to remind myself often to be more **positive**, I guess."

"How about this:

Hang this on your wall in your room and read it before you go to bed and also when you wake up.

Can you do that? You can add any pictures, stickers, or other phrases that will help you feel positive."

YOU HAVE A CHOICE

BETTER

OR

BITTER

"This is a great reminder.

It's my choice, and I choose **BETTER**.

Thanks, Marc!"

"One last thing, Josh. Before we meet next, can you make a list of 3 things you are good at?

Also, pick one area where you want to improve the most."

"Next time, we will talk about self-awareness, and how that can help you improve in the areas you are struggling with.

We will make a plan that will show you how to use your strengths to help you overcome the things you struggle with."

"Sounds like a plan. Marc! See you next time."

Now, it is your turn.

Can you write down 3 things you are really good at? They can be things you wrote earlier or new things you just thought of.

I AM GOOD AT:

1. _____

2. _____

3. _____

And one thing you struggle with that you want to improve:

I WANT TO IMPROVE:

_____

_____

_____

MY NOTES:

SELF-AWARENESS:

Know Yourself

- Meet Jill -

Next, I will meet with Jill. Jill is 12 years old and learns differently, just like Josh and me.

Jill also has a tough time in class.

She is often very tired at the end of the school day since she works so hard in class.

Jill really struggles with homework because she is too exhausted to maintain her focus.

I have been working with Jill for a short while now. I talked to her about **positive mindset** last time we met.

I shared my stories with her just as I did with Josh.

See Jill's list of things she is good at and an area she wants to improve:

I AM GOOD AT:

1. I am great in arts.

2. I enjoy playing soccer.

3. I am kind.

I WANT TO IMPROVE:

I wish I did not get overwhelmed during homework time.

I asked Jill to make a plan to use the three things she is good at to help her in the area where she struggles.

As she thinks about what she is good at, she will become more self-aware of her **strengths**. And this is what I want to talk to her about today.

First, let's see how she is doing.

I AM GOOD AT:
1. I am great in arts.
2. I enjoy playing soccer.
3. I am kind.

I WANT TO IMPROVE
I wish I did not melt down during homework time.

"Hi Jill! Tell me what you have been up to."

"Well, Marc. Things are a bit better than last time we met. I am still exhausted when I get home from school, but I feel happier."

"So glad to hear you made progress. Tell me more."

"I am trying to keep a **positive outlook** like you taught me. It was hard at first but making it a habit was a good tip.

Oh, and we won our last soccer game! I scored a goal. Life is good on that front."

GOAL!

"This ties really well into what I wanted to talk to you about today.

Have you ever heard the phrase **self-awareness**?"

"Yes, but I do not exactly know what it means."

"It means knowing yourself.
It means understanding that
how you see yourself may be
different from how others see
you.

It means recognizing your
strengths and weaknesses
and knowing how to leverage
them so you can face life's
challenges."

"Let's review the list of strengths you came up with and expand on each of them."

I am great in arts.

"I am the best artist in our grade. Miss Ling always hangs my drawings in the hall.

My art has been displayed in the Spring Art Exhibition every year."

I enjoy playing soccer.

"I may not be the best on the team, but I think I am the one that works the hardest.

I am always early for practice and run a lap or two before we start. I also practice in the park on Sundays. I even play a bit during the week in the backyard when we do not have practice because it helps my brain calm down.

Soccer makes me happy."

I am kind.

"I am a good friend. I love helping others in school.

Well, not with school work. But if they are sad or do not have a friend to hang out with, I try to include them in what I am doing so they do not feel lonely.

I think I am a good big sister as well."

"You are an amazing kid, Jill!

Sports were a strength of mine as well. I loved playing baseball and football.

That was my outlet. It was a place for me to escape from the frustration of school.

I felt in control on the field."

"My mom and dad realized focusing on my strengths was as important for my growth as my schoolwork was.

And I am so lucky that no matter how bad my grades were, they never took sports away from me.

They always encouraged me to continue working on my **strengths** and things I enjoyed."

"I was also good at giving presentations.

When I was in 6th grade English class, we had to write an essay. I knew that it was going to be very hard for me, so I asked the teacher if I could do a presentation instead.

She agreed."

"When I was your age, I felt like I had to be good at everything. Because I was not good at school, I felt like I was a failure.

I just did not see all my other accomplishments because I focused on what I was failing at. I did not take the time to look around and realize that no one was good at every single thing they did."

"That does not sound like a good strategy."

"You are right, it was not. Students that are very good in many academic subjects are the ones most rewarded in school; but the real world is not like that. We cannot be good at all we do."

"As an adult, I learned that we can be successful if we are really good at just a few things. And when we apply those skills that differentiate us from the rest, we can do well in life."

"I get it. You find your place in life and it feels like that is where you belong."

"Soccer is great but I can't think of a skill that I have that makes me stand out."

"Playing soccer is more than just kicking the ball and scoring.

You told me you run extra laps; you must be a **hard worker**."

"That means you **plan and prepare for success**.

I bet you are a **good team player** as well. This means you work great in a team or group environment.

These are definitely stand-out skills that can help you thrive!"

"Now, let's look at what you wanted to improve and how you can apply your **strengths** to get the results you want."

I wish I did not get overwhelmed during homework time.

"Tell me, how do you think you can apply your **strengths** to your homework struggle."

Plan and Prepare for Success

✓ Make a study plan and stick to it.

✓ Have snacks when I get home after school and do a bit of homework.

✓ Then, go to my soccer practice.

✓ When I get back home, do more homework, then dinner, then more work.

This will help me to break the schedule into chunks. Then, I think I will **feel less overwhelmed** and be able to **keep my attitude positive**.

Jill's Schedule	
* Have snacks when I get home * Do a bit of HW **1**	* Soccer practice **2**
* More HW when back home **3**	* Dinner *Rest of the HW **4**

MY PLAN FOR SUCCESS

My Schedule

"Wow, Jill. I am so proud of you! That sounds like a great plan. This reminds me of a quote from a famous person with a learning difference."

"Who?"

"Walt Disney!"

"The more you are like yourself,

the less you are like anyone else,

which makes you unique."

Walt Disney

"Now, since we are almost done, I want to talk about a few things you can do between now and the next time we meet."

"Oh, so more homework for me?"

"Do not worry, it is not that bad. Let's just say it is more like a game."

"I love games."

"Oftentimes, we do not realize what our strengths are because we spend too much time thinking about the things we are not good at.

This will help you become more **self-aware** and focus on your **strengths**. And these strengths will carry you to success."

FOCUS ON
STRENGTHS
NOT ~~WEAKNESSES~~

"You already picked three things you are good at. I want to expand the list.

Here is a list of things that can be your **strengths**. Just check the ones that apply to you. Then, focus on these over the next couple of weeks.

　　When do you apply them?
　　How do they help you?
　　How can you improve them?"

"Next, we will pick other areas to improve and you will have a whole toolbox filled with strengths you can use to get you the results you want.

Can you bring the list with you along with a journal next time we meet?"

"A journal and the list. Sure, I can do that, Marc. See you next time."

MY STRENGTHS

I am...

- ○ Creative
- ○ Curious
- ○ Energetic
- ○ Brave
- ○ Fair
- ○ Courageous
- ○ Adventurous
- ○ Helpful
- ○ Grateful
- ○ Compassionate
- ○ Motivated
- ○ Funny
- ○ Self aware
- ○ Imaginative
- ○ Inspirational
- ○ Persistent
- ○ Responsible
- ○ Strategic
- ○ Team-oriented
- ○ Social
- ○ Resourceful
- ○ Problem-solver
- ○ Practical
- ○ Independent

PERSEVERENCE:

Do Not Quit

- Meet Tim -

While Jill is focusing on her strengths, it is time for us to meet Tim.

You guessed it, Tim learns differently as well.

I met Tim a while back. He has come a long way and I am so proud of him.

Tim just turned 15. He is an adventurous teenager with so much going on for him. But just like Josh and Jill, he struggles in class and with homework.

Tim and I have already worked on positive mindset and self-awareness.

He has completed his strengths list...

   1. I am a leader.

   2. I love learning new things.

   3. I am brave.

...and decided where he wants to improve:

     I do not want to give up too fast even if I am not good at things.

To help Tim improve, I want to encourage him to do something that is outside his comfort zone.

I did this by asking him to start a journal and write daily entries.

I will be honest with you. Tim did not like this idea at all, and really did not want to do it. Like I said, outside his comfort zone.

Last time we met, I explained to Tim that journaling does not mean writing a ten-page essay. Just bullet points or drawings of his thoughts would be sufficient.

Plus, I did not want him to worry about his spelling, which I know is a big issue for him.

Today I am hoping he stepped up to this challenge and brought his journal with him.

Let's find out.

"Hi Tim!

I see you brought your journal
with you today. That is great!"

"I was not happy when you
asked me to write things
down in a journal. I do
enough writing at school."

"But I did what you said and just jotted down a few things, not even full sentences."

"I am so glad you gave it a shot. How did it go?"

"Well… Writing for myself was not that bad. I realized that writing when I know I am not going to be graded does not bother me as much."

I don't know what to write.

Went to the movies with Mom.

Glad my b-day is coming up.

"I made drawings like you suggested to get my thoughts on the paper. Words or images – I liked that I could do it either way."

"So, writing is difficult for you, which made you hate the idea of keeping a journal before you even tried it, is that right?"

"Yes. But the whole thing made me feel confused."

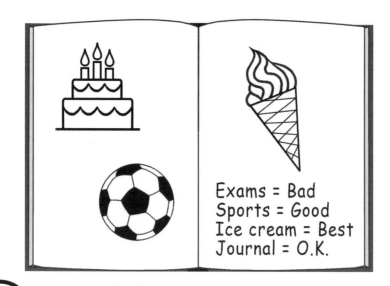

Exams = Bad
Sports = Good
Ice cream = Best
Journal = O.K.

"I realized that I almost gave up on journaling before I even tried it. But I'm glad I did not. Like I told you, I want to work on sticking with things that don't come easily.

I know that learning new things and being brave are two of my strengths. Yet, when it came to journaling, I actually felt really scared."

"So, what did you learn by trying?"

"Well, I guess I thought that my **strengths** were like an automatic thing that would just come out and help me with a challenge.

Then I remembered what you said, '*Sometimes we can be scared to do something, but we still can be brave and do it anyway.*'

Our **strengths** don't magically appear. Sometimes we have to remember to use them."

"Well, Tim, I guess you realized that we all have to work hard on our **strengths** along with our **weaknesses**. That is the only way for us to grow and improve ourselves. This is where **perseverance** – or not quitting – becomes very important."

"When I was in 9th grade, biology was so hard for me.

My teacher used confusing slides and I just did not understand the material. I could not memorize it either.

I tried so many different ways to learn the material, but nothing would stick! But you know what? I still did not give up. I kept on trying until I finally found a way that worked for me."

"What did you do?"

"I found a way to make the material relatable, which helped me remember the information better.

But if I had given up without trying many different methods, I would never have discovered the method for learning new information that I still use today."

"When you have exhausted all possibilities, remember this: you haven't."

Thomas Edison

"Let's go back to journaling. At first, you didn't want to do it because writing is difficult for you. What changed your mind?"

"I do not like writing. But I decided to try a way I had not done before.

I figured, if I tried writing in a different way, I might do better. And I did!"

"I am glad that you did not
give up. You were brave to try
a new way."

"I get what you are
saying. This really helps.

So, what should I do for
next week?"

"I would like you to pick
something else you want to
accomplish that is difficult
for you and stick with it. And
journal as well. Do you think you
can do that?"

"Definitely, Marc. See
you next time."

MY NOTES:

CONCLUSION:

Takeaways

Well, as you can see, life with a learning difference certainly comes with challenges.

But the three **Success Elements** can guide you to great strategies and help you identify the strengths that will help you succeed!

Success Element #1: Positive Mindset

Josh learned that approaching his days with a **positive mindset** will give him the motivation to keep moving forward.

The more Josh practices this positivity, the easier it will be for him to keep it up. And he always has a choice to be better or bitter.

The more he chooses **better**, the easier it will be for him to focus on the positive thoughts.

Success Element #2: Self-Awareness

In Jill's session, we talked about **self-awareness**.

The idea of understanding yourself, and the differences between that, and how others see you, can lead to real empowerment!

By the end of our session, Jill understood that taking the time to deeply examine her strengths can provide her with more tools she can use to tackle difficulties.

The more we know and understand about our abilities, the more we can put them to good use.

Success Element #3: Perseverance

Tim had a meaningful realization about **perseverance**. The strength to keep trying when things get tough is also referred to as grit.

Tim showed real grit when he decided not to quit journaling, and instead changed the way he was approaching it.

After struggling, Tim added drawings to his journal entries, which made the process much less stressful for him. He learned that giving up on journaling before he found a way that worked for him, would have been giving up on his goal.

He persevered and was able to successfully complete a task he thought was impossible for him.

Wrap Up

I see myself in all three of these kids, and in you, as well. I remember feeling helpless in school, and I remember when that feeling went from helpless to hopeful.

Once I identified the three **Success Elements** that could help me navigate the challenges ahead, I felt like I had a plan.

Every journey is made easier with a map, and I hope that this book will be the map that starts you on the road to happiness, fulfillment and success.

Just remember, you can do anything!